DREAM DIVINA'

IN NORTHW~~ESTERN~~

EUROPEAN TRADITIONS

Dream
Divination
Plants

In Northwestern European Traditions

Corinne Boyer

Illustrations by Peter Köhler

Three Hands Press

2022

First Three Hands Press edition February, 2022.

Dream Divination Plants was originally published in 2021 as a shorter monograph of the same name in the Three Hands Press 'Law of Contagion' monograph series. The present book is a revised and expanded version of that same work, with additional illustrations not included in the monograph.

Cover Image: *Night Apothecary* by Peter Köhler.

Interior Images © copyright Peter Köhler.

Book design by Joseph Uccello and Daniel A. Schulke. Typeset by JFU.

ISBN-13: 978-1-945147-45-6 (softcover)

Printed in the United States of America.

www.threehandspress.com

Table of Contents

Introduction

*...a mythical tree or vine, which has a sacredness
connected with it of peculiar significance, forming
a connecting link and medium of communication
between the world of the living and the dead. It
is generally used by the spirit as a ladder to pass
downward and upward upon...*[1]

AT THE EDGE OF SLEEP, THERE AWAITS A STRANGE
and quiet chasm. In the mind's eye, it appears as a heavy
black velvet drape within a steep ravine, its depth is a dark,
magnetic enfolding. Each evening, we are granted ingress,
and cross over into the strange realm of dreaming. This
bridge leads to separate yet integral worlds, within and
without; it represents an interface long traversed by those
seeking to understand more from the dream-realm.

1 Thiselton-Dyer, *The Mythic and Magical Folklore of Plants*, p. 537.

How have humans interacted with and found powers to influence their own dream worlds? How have they potentially changed their own Fate, by way of interference with these other worlds that are not governed by the rules of the waking world? Is it possible to do such things by way of using plant magic?

This book attempts to shed light on these inquiries, bringing together historical plant lore from Northwestern Europe. Here, the specific focus of dream manipulation is on divinatory processes. Through the lens of plant spirit-power, we find that past peoples sought prophetic knowledge by piercing the dream veil. They did this using local flora, by methods both simple and complex. This topic gives a fascinating insight into the innovation by which cultures used plants for magical purposes, and certainly hints at the vast body of knowledge existing outside the areas of the focus for the present work. Indeed, plants have been an integral part of human existence, filling needs and purposes in every area of life. It is no surprise that they were also utilized for one of the most mysterious avenues for acquiring transmissions and prophecy: the dream world.

While plant lore and specific methods for attaining prophetic dreams are at the heart of this study, the question of *why* certain plants were chosen will also be

explored. Included at the end of the book will be a section on how to make meaning from the inspirations found therein. The practice of working intimately with plant magic for general dream enhancement—including for prophecy—will be presented, growing out of years of my personal work with such processes. When we answer the questions of what plants were used, why were they used, and how they were employed, what remains is the same magnetic force, emanating from the dreaming bridge. The force which animates our hands to harvest, craft and ensorcell the plants themselves is begotten from inspirations of old. The powers of creativity and innovation are both blessings and curses—but to act upon them is the only way toward personal insight. My hope is that the information presented here will encourage appreciation of the rustic ways of times past, and rouse reflection upon the complex weaving of the dream world within one's waking reality.

A few notes on the focus and inclusion of the present research. I wish to make a distinction between dream 'enhancement' and dream *divination* in the lore. The former certainly includes the latter, however it also includes other types of dream information. Though this category is general and much less commonly found in the plant lore relating to dreams, I have included it in this work because I believe it to be relevant. Reasons to enhance or induce dreams beyond purposes of seeing future events, can include finding out information regarding some circumstance, to engaging with a specific spirit, person, plant or animal, and also for transmissions regarding magical work. However as will be seen, most historical plant lore relates to divination proper.

Passive dream divination, such as dream interpretation entries of plants, are not included. While these types of books and pamphlets have been an important source of plant lore, in particular during Victorian times, they are not included here because a preference is given to active dream-divinatory procedures. For example, a person seeking information to intentionally harvest plants and utilize them before sleeping, instead of looking up a definition about dreaming of a certain plant upon waking.

Another area of interest not included relates to dream divinations in its methods, but differs in its night-time context. This being the procedures used to bring forth visions at or around midnight, but while one is awake and not asleep. There are many methods for summoning the essence of a living person's spirit or Swedish *vålnad* (though the term often pertains to the dead) included in this category. One example is the British practice of seeing a vision of one's future spouse at midnight on Hallows' Eve by eating apple slices in front of a mirror. There are also practices and rituals that utilize sleeping for an evening before reading specific auguries, such as with removing plantain (*Plantago lanceolata*) florets wrapped in dock leaves (*Rumex obtusifolius*) and hiding them under a stone; in the morning, whether they had regrown new florets or not was an indicator of love prospects, a Scottish custom. While these kinds of traditions can be included in the category of night-induced predictions/visions, this work looks specifically to the dreaming realm for night-time omens.

Many of the methods discussed here are as simple as harvesting a specific plant and sleeping with that plant under one's pillow to see predictions in dreams. Often this was done in order to see one's future mate, essentially a love divination. Many times, it was done on an auspicious eve of the year. For example, the four-leaved clover (*Trifolium* spp.) was placed under the pillow in many parts of Europe for divinatory purposes to reveal a future spouse. Though this is the general pattern of the lore found on dream divinations coming from Northwestern Europe, there are more interesting and detailed examples as well.

While I have presented both simple and complex variations of dream divination, it is good to keep in mind the *belief* in a plant's power itself when performing such an act. The array of folk practices involving plants are thus a testament to the belief in an invisible and animistic world view that existed in the not-so-distant past. And from the examples given, we can safely assume many pieces of plant lore that seem uncomplicated are in fact missing information, in terms of additional parameters surrounding the act of plant harvest and sleep preparation.

1

The Plant Lore of Bringing a Dream

AS USING PLANTS TO ENHANCE OR 'BRING A DREAM' is indeed an ancient form of magical practice, one can be inspired by the sympathetic link between human and plant. In this wise, the plant acts to not only open the entrance to the dreaming ingress, but to somehow reveal prophetic or pertinent information by way of its enchantment and innate powers. Beyond the use by common folk for matters of love or health prognostications, it is probable that in times past these methods of 'seeing' were also done by witchcraft practitioners and those folk magicians working for clients. The village wise-person had a variety of divinatory procedures for their purposes and one of the most assessable to all would be that of the dream realm. Dreaming has long been thought to be an entrance into the spirit world, and this mysterious influence that we all encounter was no doubt called upon by those who were employed in blessing/baneful work for their communities.

While the use of utilizing dreams for prophetic knowledge has been the pursuit by those living in the past, there are still a few traditions that survive today. An example of dream divination still in place during modern times is the Scandinavian practice of placing nine different types of flowers under the pillow on Midsummer's Eve to see one's future love. Here, the number nine and the belief that prophecy is more possible on Midsummer's Eve is utilized, while the flowers themselves are various.

From Swiss lore a similar custom was observed, but with a few more details. A maiden specifically would pluck nine different flowers from nine separate places, but must include St. John's wort (*Hypericum perforatum*). Then the same operation was employed for the same purpose.[1] If St. John's wort was gathered in a ceremonial way while fasting before the sun came up on Midsummer's Day, it could be used in a dream divination relating to love by sleeping with it under the pillow. Importantly, the dew had to still be on the plant while harvesting it.[2]

1 Ibid., p. 537.
2 E. and M. A., Radford, *Dictionary of Superstitions*, p. 296.

From Aberdeenshire came the practice of gathering St. John's wort on Midsummer's Day (though it is likely this too was done before the sun came up) and sleeping with it under one's pillow in order to dream of a Saint that would give a blessing to the dreamer, keeping them safe for the coming year.[3] From Russian tradition, a total of twelve 'magical herbs' were gathered in silence and placed under the pillow on Midsummer's Eve to bring dreams. The proper words to speak were

> *John and Mary herb,*
> *head herb and all twelve herbs,*
> *tell me who my husband will be.*[4]

Related to this was placing a red rose (*Rosa* spp.) under one's pillow on Midsummer's Eve for dreams of future love.[5] Interestingly, rose has many death divinations associated with it, but not necessarily through the dream portal. A more complicated rose dream divination follows and is worth quoting in full, taken from *The Encyclopedia of*

---

3 D. C. Watts, *Elsevier's Dictionary of Plant Lore*, p. 341.
4 W. F. Ryan, *The Bathhouse at Midnight*, pp. 109–110.
5 Ibid., pp. 108–109.

Superstitions, Folklore and the Occult Sciences of the World edited by Cora Daniels and C. M. Stevens:

> Gather your rose on the 27th of June; let it be full blown and as bright red as you can get; pluck it between the hours of three and four in the morning, taking care to have no witness of the transaction; convey it to your chamber and hold it over a chaffing dish or any convenient utensil for the purpose, in which there is charcoal and sulfur of brimstone; hold your rose over the smoke for about five minutes and you will see it have a wonderful effect upon the flower. Before the rose gets the least cool, clap it in a sheet of writing paper, on which is written your own name and that of the man you love best; also the date of the morning start that has the ascendancy of that time; fold it up and seal it neatly with three separate seals, and run and bury the parcel at the foot of the tree from which you gathered the flower. Here let it remain until the 6th of July. Take it up at midnight, go to bed and place it under your pillow, and you will have a singular and eventful dream before morning or, at least before your usual time of rising. You may keep the rose under your head for

three nights without spoiling the charm. When you have done with the rose and the paper, be sure to burn them.[6]

It is interesting to note from all of the magical information in this incredible example, that July 6 is closer to Old Midsummer's Day. These dates represent roughly the 11-day difference between the Julian and Gregorian calendar change, which happened in 1582. However, England, Ireland and North America did not adopt this change until 1752 and Russia was the last to change in 1918. This explains some of the differences between 'old' Midsummer's Day and 'new', as well as for other holidays. This is also an indicator this piece of lore is quite old, along with the reference to using the chafing dish. Unfortunately, it is not dated, nor is its location of origin given.

Another Midsummer's Eve divination involves the holy oak tree (*Quercus* spp.) It was believed to have flowers that only bloomed on Midsummer's Eve, and if a maiden would lay down a white cloth under the oak tree, in the morning she would find a dusting of the pollen from the blooming flowers. If she put a pinch of this magical dust

6 Cora Linn Daniels and C. M. Stevens, *Encyclopedia of Superstitions, Folklore and Occult Sciences of the World*, pp. 837–838.

under her pillow, she would dream of her true love.[7] This reminds one of the mystical fern seed associated with Midsummer's Eve. Certainly, this was an eve where upon the witching hour of midnight, the mundane became supernatural, if only for a few moments. The same is true of the winter counterpart Christmas Eve, at midnights hour. Plants were also known to bloom uncharacteristically during this in between passage.

One method that called upon both the plant and the power of the dead was for a young maiden to gather yarrow (*Achillea millefolium*) from a young man's grave on the night of Midsummer's Eve and sleep with it under her pillow. This was sure to bring prophetic dreams of her future husband. A well-known charm from Southern England to be said while picking the graveyard yarrow leaves:

> *Yarrow, sweet yarrow, the first that I have found;*
> *In the name of Jesus Christ I pluck it from the ground;*
> *As Jesus loved sweet Mary and took her for his dear;*
> *So in a dream this night I hope my true love will appear.*[8]

7 Watts, p. 340.
8 Radford, p. 368.

A young man could do the same by picking the yarrow from the grave of a young woman in turn, likely with another incantation. The harvesting was to be done in strict silence, a rule held until retiring for the eve.[9] A combination posy for dreaming included grave yarrow, rue (*Ruta graveolens*, a plant known in different cultures to aid with the second sight) and various colored flowers, was tied together by the hairs of the woman's head whom was seeking the dream. It was then sprinkled with oil of amber using the left hand and bound to the woman's head, as she went to sleep on clean linens to receive her dream.[10]

More information about the method of collecting grave yarrow comes from South Devon. If this was done in the graveyard while the clock struck midnight, a charm was spoken:

> *Yarra, yarra, I seeks thee yarra,*
> *and now I have thee found.*
> *I prays to the gude Lord Jesus*
> *as I plucked 'ee from the ground.*

9 Folkard, p. 589.
10 Ibid., p. 589.

When the maiden returned home, she was to place the yarrow in her right stocking, tie it around her left thigh and get into bed backwards. Before falling asleep she was to speak:

> *Good night to thee yarra,*
> *Good night to thee yarra,*
> *Good night to thee yarra.*

Then three times:

> *Good night purty yarra,*
> *I pray thee sweet yarra,*
> *Tell me by the marra,*
> *Who shall me true love be.*[11]

Other variations on collecting yarrow for dream divinations come from Ireland, with the change being in the time of year and not being gathered from a graveyard. May eve or Hallows eve were also times to procure this plant for dream divinations. Making a dream pillow of sorts could be done with yarrow, sewn up in a flannel cloth. An

11 Vickery, p. 406.

incantation was to be spoken while harvesting, the most commonly referenced being:

> *Thou pretty herb of Venus tree;*
> *Thy true name it is Yarrow;*
> *Now whom my bosom friend may be,*
> *pray tell thou me tomorrow.*[12]

An Irish custom was to put the yarrow into the left stocking and tie it with the right garter.[13]

This use of yarrow for dream divination can be understood with additional information. There was belief in much protection surrounding plants that bloomed or were considered at their full power during the time of Midsummer, one of the most magical times of year for herb harvesting especially for magical operations. As the sun was at its highest point of daylight in the northern places, that solar power was transferred into the plants themselves. And there were practices with putting the leaves of yarrow over the eyes for bestowing the second sight, from the Hebrides. Because yarrow was used in the bridal bouquet in parts of Europe (though some lore states that

12 Opie and Tatem, p. 453.
13 Watts, p. 440.

it would only encourage love for seven years), and it was used to declare love from the Fens, it had associations with matters of love in general. It also was used in other kinds of divinations, as for finding out thieves and for matters of health. Finally, we cannot forget its importance in the Chinese I-Ching, an ancient divinatory system using the flowerless stalks.

Another graveyard plant used for healing spells of all sorts, was also used for prophetic dreams—grave grass. From England comes the ritual of maidens pulling three tufts of grass from a grave at the stroke of midnight on the eve of St. Mark (April 24th). After laying the grass under their pillow, this charm was repeated three times:

> *The Eve of St. Mark, by prediction is blessed,*
> *set therefore all my hopes and fears to rest;*
> *Let me know my Fate, whether weal or woe,*
> *whether my rank be high or low;*
> *Whether to live single or to be a bride,*
> *And the destiny my start doth provide.*[14]

14 Marcel De Cleene and Marie Claire Lejune, *Compendium of Symbolic and Ritual Plants in Europe*, Volume 2: p. 252.

On St. Luke's Eve, a British custom used marigold (*Calendula officinalis*), wormwood (*Artemisia absinthium*), thyme (*Thymus vulgaris*), and marjoram/oregano (*Originum vulgare*) in a potion for giving dreams of one's future husband. These herbs were to be powdered and sifted through fabric, then simmered with honey and white vinegar over a slow fire. While lying down, this mixture was used to anoint one's lips, breasts and stomach and this rhyme spoken thrice:

Saint Luke, Saint Luke, be kind with me,
In my dreams let me my true love see.[15]

There is some crossover with a few of these plants and other dream divinations. Though used for many skin maladies during both modern and olden times, few think of calendula as a plant of divination. In folklore however, it specifically concerned divination and matters of love and love magic, not only from the British Isles but also from Scandinavia. Also, from Sweden oregano tied bound to the right arm and slept upon was supposed to reveal wrongdoers in dreams.[16] This is an uncommon indication

---

15 Thiselton-Dyer, p. 72.
16 From historical Swedish Trolldom, thank you to Johannes Gårdbäck for this information.

for bringing a divinatory dream, to find out a thief, but it makes sense to include it here.

Thyme was a plant of the Faerie folk in some parts of Europe and wormwood was used to call and work with spirits of the dead. When we touch upon the threads that created this dreaming formula, delightfully prepared as a potion and anointment, the reasons of inclusion are intuitively understood. The Faerie folk of times past were not the tiny and innocent garden butterfly pixies we think of today. They were indeed small people, but could also be very large. They were also dangerous and unpredictable, thought to be much more dangerous than spirits of the human dead. Their ability to exist 'in between' realms and become invisible at will speaks to a world very much like the dream realms, one that is not fully understood by humans and yet is on the edge of everyday reality, just out of grasp.

Though typically an unlucky plant as it was associated with funerals and the ghosts of murdered people, thyme was used in a dream prediction along with rosemary. On the eve of St. Agnes of Rome (January 21) an unmarried girl would place a sprig of thyme in one shoe and a sprig of rosemary (*Rosmarinus officinalis,* currently *Salvia rosmarinus*) in the other shoe before retiring to sleep, along with one twig of each on either side of her bed. She would speak the words: *Saint Agnes that is to lover's kind, Come ease the trouble of my mind.*[17] Another source tells that the sprigs had to be sprinkled with water three times after harvesting, before placing in the shoes, which were placed on either side of the bed. A northern English and Scottish variation on the rhyme goes:

> *Agnes sweet and Agnes fair,*
> *Hither, hither now repair;*
> *Bonny Agnes let me see,*
> *the lad who will come to marry me.*[18]

Another funerary plant but also one associated with matters of love, rosemary was used in additional dream predictions. From Derbyshire, maidens would place a branch of rosemary along with a crooked six-pence under their pillows on All Hallows' Eve in order to dream of a future mate. From an 18th century chapbook, a general instruction tells to place a branch of rosemary under one's head on Easter eve in order to dream of 'the party you shall enjoy'.[19]

---

17 De Cleene and Lejune, p. 699.

18 Watts, p. 109.

19 Ibid, p. 109.

A detailed account for making a rosemary potion for dreams of one's destiny goes thus: On the Eve of St. Magdalen (July 22), three maidens under the age of twenty-one go to the bedroom chamber and prepare a potion consisting of wine, rum, gin, vinegar and water in a ground glass vessel. Each maiden then dips a sprig of rosemary in the liquid and fastens it to her bosom, also taking three sips of the potion. The three go to sleep in silence in the same bed in order to have revealing dreams.[20] Another spell including both rosemary and roses tells that on the first of July, a maiden should gather a sprig of rosemary, a white rose, a red rose, a blue flower, a yellow flower, a sprig of rue and nine blades of grass. This magical bouquet should then be bound by hairs from the head of the woman desiring dreams, and sprinkled with salt and the blood of a white pigeon. This amulet when slept with under the pillow would then reveal her future fate in dreams.[21]

To have prophetic dreams on All Hallows' Eve, a girl searched for a blackberry (*Rubus* spp.) briar grown into a hoop, crawl through it three times in the name of the Devil, and cut it in silence, taking a thorny piece home to

20 Folkard, p. 527.
21 Ibid, pp. 527–528.

sleep with it under her pillow.[22] Here we see an ill-omened plant harvested in a transgressive way in order to bring dream visions. Blackberry was associated with the Devil and dark powers in general, though it was a healing plant as well.

Another Hallows' Eve divination using apples (*Malus domestica*) for dreaming comes from Cornwall. Allan Apples were given by family and friends for good fortune in matters of love. These were large and polished apples sold by shopkeepers, meant to be used in a dream divination by sleeping with them beneath one's pillow. In the morning they were to be eaten to ensure the good omens that were hopefully given from the previous night's dreams.[23] The apple fruit/seeds were used in other ways for divination on this eve in the British Isles, such as in the Scottish 'bobbing for apples' and tossing the intact peel behind one's left shoulder at midnight in order to interpret the initial in the name of one's true love. Interestingly, from medieval times it was believed the Devil would visit young women and copulate with them in their sleep, either unwillingly or willingly, depending on the woman. As a token, he would

22 Ruth Edna Kelly, *The Book of Halloween*, p. 38.

23 Gemma Gary, *Traditional Witchcraft: A Cornish Book of Ways*, p. 189.

leave either an apple with a worm in it, or an egg next to the bed in the morning. This magical gift could be used to procure great wealth.[24] One wonders if the Devil appeared in a dream while using an apple as a divinatory tool. Apples have long held associations with enchantment, love, sex, Faerie-folk and fertility.

Though not explicitly a divination one way or another, from Cornwall comes the use of English ivy (*Hedera helix*) to bring dreams of the Devil. This was done by pinning four leaves to one's pillow-corners.[25] Ivy was an ill-omened plant not only because it was planted in graveyards (due to its evergreen quality), but because of its habit of growing in abandoned places where human habitants had once lived. It is difficult to speculate whether doing such a thing was taken on as a dare, or if the seeker involved was looking for information. Likely, both occurred.

These practices beg the question as to why a person would want to bring forth dreams of the Devil to begin with. There are a few ways in which to attempt to gain insight here, the first is that the name *Devil* very well could have been ascribed to any non-Christian deity of the past by the person recording the folklore or passing it down

24 Venetia Newell, *An Egg at Easter—A Folklore Study*, p. 70.
25 Watts, p. 211.

to another generation. Another more obvious reason to bring forth the Devil in dreams, was to utilize that power for magical transmissions and or prophecy, however most likely lore is missing from the original record in its details about the reasons why. Another line of reasoning is that it was thought that the Devil had the power to remove evil, as he himself was evil. So, once again if this was the case, lore is probably missing; we are not left with the impression that the Devil was acting as an overall positive force. The final potential reason that the Devil might be called upon in the dream realm could have been as a form of initiatory experience, as most certainly it would have been taboo and frighting to do such a thing intentionally.

Ivy was used in a love divination from the British Isles on Hallows' Eve. Nine ivy leaves were gathered and here is an Irish charm to be spoken before retiring for the eve:

Nine ivy leaves I place under my head;
To dream of the living and not of the dead;
To dream of the man I am going to wed;
to see him tonight at the foot of my bed.[26]

26 Niall Mac Coitir, *Irish Wild Plants—Myths Legends and Folklore,* p. 177.

An English version was known for men seeking to see their future wives; he was to collect ten ivy leaves and throw one behind, then sleep with the remaining nine under his pillow.

Just as seen with plants of Midsummer, the same kind of related though opposing power was carried by the evergreens of Midwinter. Holly (*Ilex aquifolium*) leaves and ivy could be put together in a charm-bundle to be slept upon on New Year's Eve for dreaming of a future spouse, the appropriate incantation to be spoken being:

> *Oh Ivy green and holly red,*
> *tell me tell me, whom I should wed.*[27]

A specific divinatory process using holly leaves comes from Northumberland. The prickly variety of holly was known as 'he-holly' and the smooth leaves variety known as 'she holly'. The 'she holly' was used, being gathered in a three-cornered handkerchief in strict silence on a late Friday eve. The person gathering the leaves had to keep silent until the following morning. Upon returning home, nine leaves were to be selected and then tied with nine knots in the three-cornered handkerchief, this charm bundle being

27 Ibid.

placed under the pillow for prophetic dreams.[28] Both holly and ivy were used in other kinds of divinations around the twelve days of Christmas, it is no surprise to find some connecting lore to bringing prophetic dreams.

Mistletoe (*Viscum album*) was no exception, as this plant of high mystical repute was believed to possess most every supernatural power known to plants, including summoning the dead to speak, neutralizing poisons, opening locks, conferring invisibility, bringing fertility and protection from lightning and fire. We find that it brings foretelling from the dream-realm as well. From Wales, mistletoe was used as a dream-amulet by sleeping with it under one's pillow. If this was done during Christmastide, it was supposed to provoke dreams of one's true love.

Additional lore tells that to bring dreams, it was to be harvested at Christmas time, specifically taken from a church.[29] If gathered on Midsummer's Eve (St. John's Eve) and placed under the pillow, mistletoe would bring dreams of either good or ill omen.[30] There was an Irish custom (although mistletoe was not native there, it did naturalize) of picking ten mistletoe berries on Christmas

28 Folkard, p. 377.
29 Marie Trevelyan, *Folklore and Folk Stories of Wales*, p. 88.
30 Mac Coitir, *Irish Wild Plants- Myths Legends and Folklore*, p. 24.

Eve, throwing the tenth one away. The remaining nine were steeped in a potion made from equal parts vinegar, honey, wine and beer. The berries were then swallowed upon retiring in order to bring prophetic dreams of one's future spouse.[31] This practice is not recommended during modern times, as the berries are known to be toxic to some degree. It is, however, a lovely example of a dream divination that involves ingestion of plants, of which there are relatively few, compared to more amuletic approaches.

The common onion was used in a dream divination on St. Thomas's Day, December 21. A maiden would peel a red onion and stick nine pins in it; the arrangement was formed of eight pins in a circle around the ninth one in the middle. This one in the middle would be named after the man the woman wanted to marry. An incantation was spoken as the pins were put in:

> *Good St. Thomas, do me right;*
> *Send me my true love tonight.*
> *In his clothes and his array,*
> *Which he weareth every day;*
> *That I may see him in the face*
> *and in my arms may him embrace.*

31 Watts, *Elsevier's Dictionary of Plant Lore*, p. 112.

The onion would be used then to invoke dreams, to be slept with under or near the pillow.[32] A Welsh custom utilizing the garden leek to bring dreams of one's future spouse instructs to go into the garden and pluck the leek out of the ground with one's teeth. This was placed under the pillow before retiring.[33]

In keeping with the practice of using what was readily available for magical purposes, lemons were used in a unique way to bring dreams to a woman of a desired man, to foretell the fate of the situation. From a manual dating 1760, the instructions tell: the woman was to peel two lemons and place the skins under her armpits for the entire day. Before going to bed, she would rub them onto the four corners of her bedstead. The man in question was hoped to be seen bringing lemons to her that eve in a dream; if not, all hope was lost for the situation.[34]

The bay tree (*Laurus nobilis*) was used for prophecy since ancient times. A branch of it was used in Grecian magic for revealing that which was hidden and the tree itself was believed to cause sleep and visions. Sleeping upon the boughs was known to bring true visions to soothsay-

32 Ibid, p. 112.
33 Ibid, p. 108.
34 Opie and Tatem, p. 231.

ers and prophets.[35] From Lincolnshire to bring dreams of one's future mate, five bay leaves were pinned to one's pillow; one in each corner and one in the middle.[36] One variation comes from Devon. On St. Valentine's Eve this was done, but the charm was also spoken seven times, while counting to seven, seven times over each interval:

Sweet guardian angels let me have,
what I most earnestly do crave—
A valentine endued with love,
who will both true and constant prove.[37]

From the work of Albertus Magnus, a charm that kept one from slander also had the power of revealing a thief in dreams when slept with under the pillow; marigold (*Calendula officinalis*) gathered while the sun was in Leo in August, wrapped in a bay leaf with a wolf's tooth was the prescribed combination.[38]

A Russian example uses Eastern pasque flower (*Pulsitilla patens*) known as the 'Dream Herb' or *Son-trava*.

35 C. J. S. Thompson, *Magic and Healing*, p. 113.

36 De Cleene and Lejune, Vol. 1, p. 132.

37 Vickery, *A Dictionary of Plant Lore*, p. 28.

38 Michael R. Best and Frank H. Brightman, *The Book of Secrets of Albertus Magnus*, pp. 4–5.

Its gorgeous blue flowers were slept with under the pillow to bring dreams, and it was known that what was seen in dreams would then come true.[39] Medicinal uses of this plant include it as a sedative and sleeping aid.[40] This use for dreaming however is an older use and no longer widely known about.

Seeds feature in a few dream divinations. Opium poppy seeds (*Papaver somniferum*) were used on the eve of St. Andrew, November 30th by a young woman who wanted to see her future spouse. She would sprinkle the seeds over her body before sleeping.[41] Flax seeds (*Linum usitatissimum*) were either placed under pillows or scattered in the bed in order to produce dreams of future husbands. One incantation spoken while doing so from Mecklenburg went:

Here I sow my flax, here I sow my seed;
If there is someone who loves me,
then may he appear in my dream at night.[42]

39 Folkard, p. 107.
40 Thank you to Victoria Boyer for this information.
41 De Cleene and Lejune Volume 2, p. 484.
42 Ibid, p. 237.

Seeds such as linen, hemp and dock are also used in love divinations that produce visions at night, hence the use of them for the dream realms as well. A related Russian method was for a woman to sprinkle herself with oats (*Avena sativa*) before going to bed, and to recite *Intended one, come to tend your garden,* or alternatively *Intended one, come to reap your oats.*[43] In the past, seeds were utilized as a draw and distraction for keeping wandering spirits of the dead occupied by way of counting. This seems to be the same logic that is brought into these examples, though with the intent of drawing the spirit part of a living person instead. Also, the obvious connection of fertility to the seeds used comes to mind when understanding these simple and yet helpful ways of yesteryear.

Pine (*Pinus spp.*) was used for bringing prophetic dreams. A pine tree from Scotland on the Isle of Bute was called a *Dreaming Tree.* The needles were collected with some sort of ceremony for making and placing a charm under the pillow to bring dreams of a future husband or wife.[44] The pine, though funerary in nature, is a cone/seed bearing tree with many fertility and healing associations from times past. As with numerous edible nut/fruit/seed

43 Ryan, *The Bathhouse at Midnight*, p. 103.
44 Watts, p. 108.

producing trees such as oak, hazel, apple, and walnut, we find love, fertility and sexual connections in the lore and traditions employed.

Another 'Tree of Dreams' was considered to be the elm (*Ulmus spp.*). The ill-omened elm however was a tree associated with the dead, as it does not bear fruit and can be quite long lived. From Virgil we read:

In the midst a gloomy Elm displays its boughs and
aged arms, which seat vain dreams are commonly
said to haunt, and under every leaf they dwell.[45]

Indeed, the forlorn elm has been known as the 'Tree of
Morpheus', and the souls of the dead were conceived of as
dreams and birds, from old Italic lore, finding residence
within the elm tree.[46]

Though both Elder (*Sambucus nigra*) and Hazel (*Cor-
ylus avellane*) have the power of second sight and divinatory prowess bestowed upon them in particular for dealing
with supernatural spirits, there are but a few uses for the
dreaming realm. Sleeping under a hazel tree was thought
to produce prophetic dreams, a piece of lore from 1930.[47]
This simple yet brave act to bring forth dreams is mirrored
in lore from the Native Americans on the west coast in
the example of sleeping under western red cedar (*Thuja
plicata*) to bring wild dreams.[48] With the English walnut

---

45 Alexander Porteous, *The Forest in Folklore and Mythology*, Dover
   Publications, 2002 (1928), p. 202.
46 Lewis Bayles Paton, *Spiritism and the Cult of the Dead in Antiquity*,
   Restoration Editors reprint, 2017 (1921), p. 76.
47 De Cleene and Lejune Volume I, p. 311.
48 See Daniel Moermans *Native American Medicinal Plants* and
   look under the heading *Psychological Aid* for a few other scat-

(*Juglans regia*) there is the warning that though sleeping under the tree could bring prophetic dreams of one's true love, death could also occur as the tree was associated with the dead, evil spirits and the Devil in olden times in parts of Europe. Hazelnuts burned and the ashes placed in 'packets' were supposed to bring happy dreams when placed under the pillow.[49] Here we begin to enter into the ways of plants when encountering the Nightmare, another branch of oneiric lore.[50]

A divination concerning the elder tree was to place a branch beneath one's pillow; it was believed that it would foretell in dreams what would happen during the months that the elder was in flower, typically around Midsummer.[51] The elder tree had different formulas and prescriptions when 'seeing' and finding out both witches and Faeries, typically the green rind was used or the tree itself

tered interesting dream uses.

49 Daniels and Stevens, *Encyclopedia of Superstitions, Folklore and Occult Sciences of the World*, Volume 1, p. 223.

50 For information about plants that were historically used for keeping away nightmares, see my book The Witches Cabinet, Three Hands Press, 2021: *By Chaplet and Spirit Smoke: Plants used Against Nightmares and Haunted Sleep.*

51 Ibid., p. 231.

visited on Midsummer's Eve at midnight for visions of the Hidden Folk.[52]

One piece of lore from Sweden tells to sleep with a bouquet of mugwort (*Artemisa vulgaris*) under the pillow in order to dream of one's future spouse.[53] Medieval lore acknowledges the same, that by sleeping with a bag of mugwort under one's pillow, prophetic dreams would be revealed.[54] Other lore from the British Isles utilizes mugwort as a supernatural 'dreaming coal'. On Midsummer's Eve, certain plants were believed to have buried beneath them a magical 'coal', likely a blackened root. As with the otherworldly fern seed, it was supposed to glow at midnight, the time of harvest. Along with plantain (*Plantago* spp.) and burdock (*Arctium lappa*), mugwort was one of the plants onto which this phenomenon occurred. While the coals from these plants gathered at midnight on this auspicious eve were endowed with specific healing properties, the mugwort coal was used as a dreaming amulet to

52 For both hazel and elder lore relating to the second sight, see my article "*Plants and the Second Sight—An Investigation into Perceiving the Hidden*" (2019).

53 From historical Swedish Trolldom, special thanks to Johannes Gårdbäck for this information.

54 Elbee Wright, *Book of Legendary Spells*, Marlar Publishing, 1974 (1968), p. 159.

see future spouses in a dream.[55] With the popularity during modern times of using mugwort for a dreaming herb, it is surprising there is not more lore to be found relating to sleep and dreams; much of mugwort's lore involves protection from evil spirits and the Evil Eye.[56]

For enhancing dreams, spurge laurel (*Daphne laureola*) interestingly was listed from Johann Weyer in *De praestigiis Daemonum et incantationibus et Veneficiis* from 1568 in connection with divinatory practice known as *daphnomancy,* ascribed to demonic powers. The divination was to burn the toxic leaves in a fire while scrying into the smoke and flames. And the leaves were known to be put under

55 Daniels and Stevens, Vol. 2, p. 819. See also Opie and Tatem, pp. 89–90.

56 The 'Evil Eye' as it is known, was and is a cross-cultural and universal spiritual affliction that is caused by specifically the emotion and power of envy. In times past and in certain parts of the world today, jealousy of a neighbor, friend or family member was believed to cause sickness, whether intentionally applied or not. This was thought to be cast on the victim, by way of a 'poisonous' glance of the eyes. Most times, the person with the power of the Evil Eye was not doing it intentionally. Often strong-willed individuals, red heads, people with eye abnormalities and of course witches, were through to have this power. Usually the young, the old, the compromised and animals were most effected. But crops, land, homes and love relationships could be affected by this feared enchantment.

the pillow to induce dreams.[57] The poisonous sap was also used for invisible ink, as can be done with fig sap.

The lucky white variety of heather (*Calluna vulgaris*) was placed under the pillow by one that wanted to dream.[58] In the past, the white flowers were more rare than the usual pink, so this use makes sense for a plant that already had Faerie associations on the British Isles. To have dreams of beloved or absent ones, the roots of English daisy (*Bellis perennis*) were placed under the pillow, a use from 1696.[59] With all of the love associations with this plant, it is not hard to see where this use comes from. From England, to dream of future lovers, maidens would place daisies under the pillow and hang shoes outside their windows.[60]

57 Watts, p. 107.
58 De Cleene and Lejune, Vol. 2, p. 326.
59 Folkard, p. 308.
60 De Cleene and Lejune, Vol. 1, p. 220.

2

Practical Applications of the Lore

WITHIN MANY EXAMPLES of the flora that was utilized for prophetic dreaming, and before sharing some personal findings on the subject, it is useful to consider the overwhelming magical intent common to much of the lore—love divination. It is helpful to remember that in times past, the Fate-given selection of one's mate was in all manner of ways crucial for survival, for either party involved. People had far fewer options, hence the large amount of love magic that was utilized and thus preserved. It is difficult to imagine in modernity such limitations, and being confined to a small area and population, at least in comparison to today in the western world. For better or worse, it is clear by the amount of plant lore used to bring dreams of future spouses how widespread these practices were.

Plants can be considered to be one branch of folklore relating to dream divinations; this work does not consider examples of dream divinations working with other *materia magica* or methods, such as the Scandinavian 'Dream Pancake'; the use of extra salt in pancakes (also in porridge and eggs, depending on the culture) for revealing love prospects. The importance of manipulating one's dreams to see the future, in particular on nights when the veil between the spirit world and the mundane world was thin, was a way to bring hope and make sense of stressful circumstances for ancestors of the past. Though the severity may be on a different scale, our reasons for doing such things in modern times are not so very different than those who have walked before.

To move past working with dreams solely for purposes of love, the dark chasm that lies beneath the dreaming bridge can be interfered with for prophetic dreams of all sorts, as both lore and practice indicate. Any question that the dreamer asks of the dream can potentially be provided with an answer or a prophecy—only time will reveal to what degree the interpretation becomes as such. All people have at least a few prophetic dreams in a lifetime. It is one thing to have a few in number, it is another thing to be able to control and work with prophecy in the dreaming realms on a regular basis—or any other form of divination for that matter. Purpose, practice and perseverance are in my experience, as important as a natural gift in dreaming ability, memory and interpretation. And even a slight inclination toward being a strong dreamer can be tended to bring forth an intimacy with the facets of the complex, dark glittering jewel that is the limitless dream realm.

Guidelines for developing a strong dream-practice are not the heart of this work, but as it is a helpful backbone on which to integrate divinatory allies such as plants into certain methods at certain times, a few keys will be mentioned. Handwriting dreams in a dedicated book with dates, times and details is essential for not only record keeping and revisiting, but also for insight into the patterns of dream types and frequency. Many people disdain recording dreams of the mundane variety; however, when learning about one's own dreaming process, and for strong recall, it is necessary. The resistance to doing so can be remarkable, but when done enough and when recall is solid, mundane dreams can be fished out, noted and discarded against the more desirable dreams which are recorded. These favored dreams remaining, though fewer in number, are the kinds of dreams that include prophecy and have the potential to answer the questions of the seeker, by way of revelation with symbols, archetypes, motifs and patterns that is in the language only the dreamer can understand.

Often prophetic dreams are cryptic, and only on occasion direct and obvious. Part of what I find particularly fascinating with the dream realm is that no one besides the dreamer can make meaning, which is where the art of interpretation becomes as personal revelation, and is gained only by experience, time, effort and observance. It remains a uniquely individual process where there is a strange world of 'dream memories' and associations, places, images, beings, objects, and realizations that cannot be articulated with any language to another human, scarcely even to oneself. When working with dreams, it is helpful to leave books behind and engage fully in the received material instead.

After many years of working with my own dreams, working with practices traditional and improvised, it is my conclusion that using the *materia magica* of plants to assist in manipulating dreams is generally unreliable. In my experience it has about a thirty percent effectiveness rate, in terms of enhancements or transmissions or questions being answered; and this may or may not be repeatable using the same means. This seems to be true among myself and students whom I work with. However, this does not mean these methods are not of value. Below are the reasons why working with the human will to influence dreams should not be abandoned at first glance with these seemingly discouraging results —though one out of three times is favorable when all variables are taken into account. Probability factors are not that straightforward; if one tries using plants for dream divination, perhaps it would take ten times to have an effect. And then the results could be a success three times in a row. Then we return to a long stretch of no noticeable effect.

The consideration of factors affecting one's dreams must be mentioned. Mundane influences such as seasons, day light, moon phase, hormones/menstrual phase, stress levels, darkness/sound factors, sleep interruption, bed sharing, nutrition/medication effects, illness, substance use and individual sleep patterns/practices bring many 'wild cards' into the game, factors that are hard or impossible to control. There are also magical influences, spirit-powers, and invisible factors that play a part. By deciding to willingly interfere with one's own dreaming process, it is helpful to remember that integrating the use of a plant/ method to affect the overall dreaming jewel, we are but alighting one facet of a whole system intentionally mysterious to penetrate by most means.

Paradoxically, the age-old tendency to wake during night for various reasons helps with dream recall greatly. If, for example, one is awakened to tend babies or children, or animals that are about to birth, or feed the fire for a sick person, it is very helpful for getting an immediate glimpse of dream information that would most likely be lost otherwise. I have found it to be true with students, that those who sleep the entire night through do not have as many dreams to report. This can be artificially manipulated by use of an alarm clock, set at least once around the 2-3 am. However undesirable this may seem, it can bring forth the hidden fruit of dreams, if one is willing to record what is remembered during this time.

The reasons for using plants to induce prophetic dreams include bringing awareness of a specific plant's powers, and to be closer with the chosen plant, even if a dream is not given in the timeframe sought. In truth, anything that is ritually worked with will become known in a less straightforward manner to the beholder, due to nuance and numen. The chance to observe subtleties of the plants in question is always the advantage of working with them, no matter what the outcome. The *materia magica* therefore enhances the dreaming experience, more as a lens than for the end result. The most important predictor of success is Fate and relationship. Fate of when a divinatory message comes in a dream is something beyond the scope of this work- but as with all divinatory processes, there are times we get to peer into the veil, and times we do not. Relationship with the plant is the paramount factor; to invite the *daemon* of the plant into one's dreams, it helps immensely to have enchantment and experience with that plant beforehand.

The power of belief is another factor. One's own mind and ability to be affected is important, as in what plants are used, the ways and details of preparation and the unconscious willingness to open up to the nighttime interaction. As an example, if one believes that an elixir taken internally will be more effective than hanging a chaplet above the bed, it is wise to start with those intuitive insights.

Along with many ideas and inspirations that are revealed in the previous lore, here are suggestions for the ways in which plants can be used in the bedroom chamber, before retiring and to effect one's dreams. Making a ritual charm for either hanging above the bed near the head, wearing as an amulet around one's neck, or sleeping with under the pillow is a straightforward way to be 'close to the plant'. Dried or fresh plant material can be used by itself or with other additions. A recommendation is to try individual plants alone and work with the charm every other night for a week. It is helpful to compare and contrast the effects on both nights employed and not. If an initial ritual is created for consecrating the amulet done on an eve of power, the utilized incantation can be repeated on subsequent nights before sleep and appropriate offerings made.

Hanging a bouquet or chaplet of a fresh plant near the head or placing in a vase near the bed is another method to try. There are occasional warnings in folklore against sleeping with certain flowers in the room, such as with linden (*Tilia europaea*). From Germany, it was thought that the fragrance from linden flowers would bring erotic dreams to girls,[1] similarly we see the same warning with honeysuckle (*Lonicera pericylmenum*) from Finland.[2] It can be elaborated here that these flowers can be tried for such purposes if desired, however it is advised to start with small amounts of such fragrant plants. Lilies (*Lilium spp.*) for example have compounds that can cause headaches for some people. The fragrance of a wilting plant becomes stronger than one kept fresh in water, for a number of hours then dramatically declines. However, some plants that are night blooming, such as Dames Rocket (*Heperis matronalis*), are stronger smelling during the evening time.

The aroma from fresh plants is a powerful way to work with them for dreaming purposes. Fragrant leaves can be harvested and placed in cotton bags for use near the head or under the pillow. This brings to mind the Romany use of fresh spearmint (*Mentha spicata*) placed in bags and

1 Watts, p. 229.
2 Ibid, p. 198.

slept near for the purposes of clearing up allergies and the original 'dream pillow' from Ireland, using only hops (*Humulus lupulus*) as a sleeping aid. There are about ten percent of people in my experience who cannot have fresh mugwort in their rooms at all, as it causes unwanted, disturbing dreams. For others, it does hardly a thing. An important reminder is that what works for some does not work for all.

Bringing hawthorn flowers in the house during the month of May and falling asleep with them in the room was supposed to bring great misfortune, lore from Suffolk.[3] Hawthorn was known to be a tree of the Faerie, and white flowers were in general associated with death and funerals, perhaps the logic here. The same was said about falling asleep under the tree itself. There are numerous ill-omened plants that give warnings in the lore about sleeping in their shade—English ivy, walnut, elder are a few other examples. To sleep in a field of fava beans (*Vicia faba*) in flower was said to bring madness, nightmares and death.[4] This brings forth another method when working with dreams and plants—to sleep under or next to the living plants being investigated. Undertaking this method

3 Ibid, p. 182.
4 De Cleene and Lejune, Vol. 2, p. 73

has initiatory components and is not for the faint of heart! However, a milder version can be gleaned while taking naps during the daytime hours. Often, a marked impression is made, and some sort of transmission bestowed, even in the fleeting sleep that comprises a daylight slumber.

Ingestion and anointment are additional ways to be in contact with the plant in a more physical and sensual manner. For ingestion, infused port or brandy with the dried or fresh plant is recommended. The dosage can be taken similar to a general tincture dose (20–35 drops or two dropperfuls) when dealing with plants that are not considered toxic or low dose. But even 5–10 drops, or a full dropperful taken just before retiring can be sufficient. A tea made from the plant is best if prepared with a small amount of liquid to avoid unnecessary trips to the bathroom. Though it is worth noting that in particular for people that have trouble remembering dreams, one of the previously mentioned techniques is to set an alarm and wake in the middle of the night, thus byway of interrupting ones sleep cycle, one catches the dream before it fades into the next round.

Anointing with an infused oil or a salve of a plant can be a pleasant way to enjoy the aroma and effects while passing into the dream realm. Depending on the plants involved, anointing can be sparse or copious. Making a strong tea of the plant and using it in a bath or a footbath is also a method to be tested. All of the physical ways to take in the plants are certainly more inspired with ritual components included, such as with incantations, spirit summoning, offerings and altars. Burning fumigations of plants in the darkened chamber is one of the most sensual methods, not to mention traditional when it comes to invocation of spirit power. The inclusion of fire to transform the plant into smoke has its own genius and practice. More care must be taken here, for obvious reasons of having proper ventilation and attention to the vessel which perfumes the space with smoke.

When making an herbal bath for dreaming purposes, it is helpful to first make 'bath tea' upon the stovetop in order to achieve a therapeutic aromatic experience. Simply adding plant to warm bathwater alone is a waste of plant material in my opinion, and will not bring out the full potential of the plants' powers. Nor will the mere use of essential oils. More heat is needed in order to make a stronger water extract, so 1–2 cups of the dried or freshly chopped plant can be added to 6–8 cups of water on the stovetop, brought to a full rolling boil with the lid on, and allowed to steep for at least an hour. This then can be strained directly into the bath, with no future mess to clean up. For a ritual bath for one seeking dreams, it is recommended that some of the traditional observances of magic be adhered to: strict silence during and after the bath, no engaging with another person in any manner and in this case, going directly to bed after bathing. If prayers are the be uttered, keep them quiet and out of hearing by others nearby.[5]

When implementing any of these methods for plant spirit influence upon one's dreams, it is helpful after whatever procedure is undertaken, to fall into sleep with the intent and the plant essence within the mind's eye. Indeed, purely envisioning a plant as one crosses the dreaming bridge into the wild terrain of night and otherness can itself be the spiritual medicine that one is seeking. This done with prayers of intent, repeated like a concentrated lullaby, is sufficient at times to cause prophetic dreams. And as in the lore, to choose traditional eves when spirit-powers are heightened is an important consideration. In practice however, this can be limiting; therefore, using the eve before a dark or full moon adds endowment to any dreaming procedure.

5 Strong decoctions of fresh flowers may be added to the bath as a means of inducing dreams, such as Mugwort, Rose, Orange Blossom or Saucer Magnolia (*Magnolia soulangeana*). 1–2 gallons of the concentrated decoction is added to 30 gallons bathwater. The author thanks Daniel A. Schulke for these suggestions.

3

Conclusion

TO ACQUIRE INFORMATION FROM DREAMS IS ONE thing; to work successfully with that information in waking life is another. In many respects, what is done with the information after the dream makes it meaningful in mundane and magical endeavors. Through dreams we can learn a great deal about our deeper feelings, fears, and desires. We can look within in the black mirror, and see the spirits pursuing us by repeat incidence. *Materia magica* can be gathered in the dream land, just as it is in the local forests and meadows. There are transmissions gifted, wisdom bestowed, and contact with the beloved dead restored. There are warnings and omens, for good and ill. It is another world that is waiting every night, to be glimpsed and savored. As a strangely-vinted wine it is to be sipped, each small draught another flavor on the palate.

Perhaps the dream divination plants act as keys to a doorway, opening or keeping closed that which lies beyond. And as with all acts of divination, the inquiries beg the question—do we truly want to see that which waits behind the door? When plants are used for any work requiring revelation, be it truth-telling, bringing visions, procuring far-sighted dreams, breaking enchantments, they likely aid in indirect ways as well, such as with grounding and helping one withstand what is shown.

Pursuit of knowledge through the dreamscape is one of the most ancient ways of receiving magical teachings. The night-woven messages that come through dreams are dark gifts touched by the intoxication of sleep, silver of moonlight, and the dust of moth wings. In the spirit-haunted world of magic, they are presented within the arms of the dead, the witch's plants and night creatures. Such methods, when informed by spirit, bring forth power, like a summoned ghost of old—speaking in riddles, and yet containing the answers for those with eyes to see them.

Appendix

Recipes for Bringing a Dream

Below I include a few personal recipes and spells for assisting in bringing dreams. These are some of the most helpful in my experience, with the first three being the most useful according to my students specifically focusing on plants and dreams. I hope that they will be of use for the practical work of dream divination with plants.

Mugwort Salve

To make an infusion of *Artemisia vulgaris*, it is best to harvest the plant in full bud/flower during August when the essential oils are high. A fresh infused oil can be made, but it is also possible to make a fragrant oil from the dried material, if it was harvested and dried during the optimum time, though the method in making it is different. Once the oil is made, the salve may be made in turn.

For making a fresh mugwort-infused oil, harvest the plant in bud/flower; the better if near or on the eve of the full moon. Let the plant wilt for 4–6 hours and strip the leaves and buds/flowers from the thick stalk. If processing a lot of material, it is recommended to wear leather gloves, as the oils will certainly be absorbed into the hands. If one is sensitive, wash hands immediately after this step, or just wear the gloves. Cut the material up using heavy kitchen shears and place in a mason jar, so that the plant material fills about ¾ of the jar, not packed. Fill the jar with extra virgin olive oil and each day for 2–4 weeks, expose the plant to about an hour or two of hot sun per day. It is also necessary to stir the oil each day, to prevent mold from growing on top.

After the oil is finished, strain the plant material through a sieve and measure the oil. Reserving the oil, you will now combine it with beeswax for the salve. For each cup of mugwort oil, use 1 oz. of beeswax cut small, or bought in bead form. Beeswax is also easy to break up with a hammer if frozen and wrapped in paper. This must be heated with the oil in a double boiler until melted, and then poured into small tins or jars until hardened.

To use the salve before retiring to bed, rub some on the chest, the soles of the feet and the palms. This is often enough to notice its effects. But if one is sensitive, start with just the palms of the hands.

Elderflower Infused Port and the Elder Flower Locket

This recipe is simple and delicious. Take dried elder flower (*Sambucus nigra*) and fill any size mason jar a little less than halfway. Pour good quality port wine over the flowers and fill the jar, sealing it. The dried flowers will soon absorb the port. Shake every day for a month. This can be made on the eve of the full moon if so desired. Strain after a month, being sure to push the liquid out of the flowers. Reserve the port in an embellished bottle, and keep it near the bedside. A small shot before sleeping is sure to be a delight to the senses and help one find the entrance to the dream world.

Another easy but effective way to use dried elder flowers is to powder the material by pushing it through a sieve using a wooden pestle. Take this powder and wrap it in a small piece of wax paper and then place it within a locket. Before sleep, remove the powder and take a pinch into the mouth for a delicious elder flavor. A plant of the moon but Saturnian in nature, this witch-tree is a helpful ally in seeing into the dark dreams that waiting on the edges of sleep.

Yarrow Elixir

This elixir can be made with fresh or dried yarrow (*Achillea millefolium*) flowers and leaves. I find that I slightly prefer the dried version. But this must be made with home-dried plant material, gathered during the Midsummer tide, dried properly and processed before it fades. If good quality home dried material is not available, then fresh plant in full flower is preferred.

Fill a mason jar of any size halfway with dried, crumbled leaf and flower, or three-fourths of the way with fresh-chopped leaf and flower. Then fill the jar to three quarters with a good quality unflavored brandy. Fill the remainder with honey, leaving an inch of shaking room on top. Shake every day for a month and strain.

Keep in a small dropper bottle near the bedside. Take two dropperfuls before sleep, or one dropperful in the night upon waking. This is a very helpful elixir for bringing dreams, prophetic or not.

Moth Apple Charm

A beautiful charm with a red apple and dried moths can be made in the autumn time, in particular if one wants to bring dreams of ancestors. Near to, or on All Hallow's Eve, procure a red apple and cut it in two. Three small dried moths (these can easily be found on window sills and near the porch lights during late summer already expired, and taken and dried fully for later use). Place the moths within the cut apple, joining the two halves together again by using a few broken toothpicks. Before retiring or nearest midnight, speak appropriate incantations over the apple, asking it to bring forth dreams. Sleep with the apple as near to the pillow as possible, ideally in the bed.

Dreaming Oil

A dreaming oil can be made by first finding a small bottle that has silver inlay. Once gently cleaned and dried, fill this bottle halfway with dream *materia magica*. Things to include can be datura seeds *Datura stramonium* spp., cut up owl feathers, dried mugwort *Artemisa vulgaris*, dried moths, dried white rose petals *Rosa spp.*, dried elder flowers *Sambucus nigra*, and any other personal items connected to dreams. Then pour in extra virgin olive oil. Cork the bottle and do not use for a full moon cycle. Keep it in moonlight as much as possible for this next month, which may mean making it a certain time of year when the moon is most visible in your area. Also keep it outside during the time of the dark moon. After that is done, it is ready for use. It never needs to be strained (hence using only dried materials to prevent molding and not overfilling it) but can be used to anoint night working items and also one's temples before sleep. It is a strange oil to be certain, but one that is strengthening to ones dream work if used on occasion.

Mandrake Root as Dreaming Companion

One use for the notorious mandrake root (*Mandragora officinarum*) is to work with it as a dreaming companion. In my experience of working with mandrake, each root is a different *daemon* and its powers cannot be guessed at before encountering it upon harvesting and spending time with that particular plant. But if one is attempting to make a connection to a root after harvesting, through courting and trance work, an indicator that it can be used for dream work will come in the form of a dream about the root itself. Once the dream is brought forth, one can make a place for the root at the bedside on a small altar of red silk. It is wise to surround the root with iron, for protection from it when not in use. It is no small thing to keep a mandrake at the bedside, and have it watch over one's sleep.

When dreams are desired, it is time to wake the root by way of specific offerings and prayers, and by removing the iron that is closest to the bed, for the night. This unleashes the mandrake and allows it to enter into one's dream states. In the morning, gratitude is to be given no matter what the outcome, and the iron replaced. It is not recommended to work with this kind of mandrake more than once per month.

Opium Poppy and Snake Ash Charm

The opium poppy (*Papaver somniferum*) is in its medicine and symbology aligned with sleep and dreaming.

The whole heads can be hung, once emptied of their seeds (which will spill all over) above the bed in a chaplet style, bound with a black ribbon. This can be removed when not in use and stored in black cloth in a cupboard. The seeds, saved and dried, can be mixed in equal part snake ash to be wrapped in white silk and worn as an amulet while sleeping in order to bring prophetic dreams.

Snake ash was used in the traditional Swedish sorcery of *Trolldom* for many things, but one way to use it from Danish lore was to bind it to the head in order to bring foretelling dreams. The traditional way that it was made will not be included here, but a simplified and more humane version can be used. A dead snake is to be found, all the better if it is a viper. This is to be burned on a fire of fir wood and then pulverized in an iron mortar and pestle to render it to a powder. This can be stored indefinitely in a glass vial and used as needed. It blends very well with poppy seeds for bringing dreams.

White Heather and Grave Earth Charm

White heather (*Calluna vulgaris*) can be harvested on the eve before the full moon, if possible under the cover of night and moonlight, without the use of iron. This herb is to be dried near the hearth and then combined with graveyard earth in a bundle of either black or white cloth, then placed under the pillow to bring dreams of the dead. White is used for ancestral dead, black is used for beloved dead. As historically white flowers were used for funerals and wakes, white lilies can be substituted here especially when wanting to bring dreams of the beloved dead.

Bibliography

Best, Michael R. and Frank H. Brightman eds. *The Book of Secrets of Albertus Magnus.* Weiser Books, 1999, (1550).

Boyer, Corinne. "Plants and the Second Sight—An Investigation into Perceiving the Hidden" *Verdant Gnosis* Vol. 5. Revelore Press, 2019.

Daniels, Cora Linn Daniels and C. M. Stevens. *Encyclopedia of Superstitions, Folklore and Occult Sciences of the World.* Volume 2, Gale Research Co. 1971 (1903).

De Cleene, Marcel and Marie Claire Lejune. *Compendium of Symbolic and Ritual Plants in Europe, Volume 1: Herbs.* Man and Culture Publishers, 2003 (1999).

——— *Volume 2: Trees and Shrubs.*

Folkard, Richard. *Plant Lore, Legends and Lyrics.* Forgotten Books, 2012 (1892).

Gary, Gemma. *Traditional Witchcraft: A Cornish Book of Ways.* Troy Books, 2015 (2008).

Kelly, Ruth Edna. *The Book of Halloween.* Forgotten Books, 2011 (1919).

Mac Coitir, Niall. *Irish Wild Plants—Myths Legends and Folklore.* The Collins Press, 2008.

Newell, Venetia. *An Egg at Easter—A Folklore Study.* William Clowes and Sons Limited, 1971.

Opie, Iona and Moira Tatem. *A Dictionary of Superstitions.* Oxford University Press, 1989.

Radford, E. and M. A. *Dictionary of Superstitions.* Metro Books, 1961 (1948).

Ryan, W. F. *The Bathhouse at Midnight,* The Pennsylvania State University Press, 1999.

Thiselton-Dyer, T. F. *The Mythic and Magical Folklore of Plants.* Samhain Song Press, 2008 (1889).

Thompson, C. J. S. *Magic and Healing.* Bell Publishing, 1989 (1946).

Trevelyan, Marie. *Folklore and Folk Stories of Wales,* Reprint EP Publishing Limited, 1973 (1909).

Vickery, Roy ed. *A Dictionary of Plant Lore,* Oxford University Press, 1995.

Watts, D. C. *Elsevier's Dictionary of Plant Lore,* Academic Press, 2007.

Wright, Elbee. *Book of Legendary Spells.* Marlar Publishing, 1974 (1968).